A+ books

Measure It!

How Do You Measure
Liquids?

by Thomas K. and
Heather Adamson

CAPSTONE PRESS
a capstone imprint

Tim and his mom are back from walking the dog. Everyone is thirsty.

Who has the most water?

Different shapes can make measuring liquid tricky. Tim tries a ruler. The blue sport bottle is taller than the orange one. But rulers only show how tall or how deep something is.

3

Tim needs to measure how much, or the amount of, liquid. He needs a container.

He fills the blue sport bottle all the way. Then he pours all the water into the orange bottle. But the orange bottle doesn't fill up.

The orange bottle is shorter, but it holds more.

4

Tim then fills up the orange bottle and pours it into the dog bowl. **Uh-oh.** The water doesn't fit. The dog bowl holds less water.

Tim's orange bottle had the most water!

Mom asks, "How many cups are in the orange bottle?"

Tim thinks. Which cup? A coffee cup? A sippy cup? They're cups, but they don't hold the same amount.

Mom meant a measuring cup.
People have made standard tools so
everyone can measure the same way.
Measuring spoons, cups, and pitchers
have marks to show amounts of liquid.

We measure liquids by pouring them into the tool. Put the measuring container on a level spot. Get down low so your face is even with the container.

Look at the lines on the side.

People use cups, pints, quarts, or gallons to measure large amounts of liquid.

For smaller amounts, use teaspoons, tablespoons, and fluid ounces.

1 gallon =
4 quarts

½ gallon =
2 quarts

1 quart =
2 pints

The metric system uses milliliters and liters to measure liquid. In this book, metric measurements are shown in parentheses next to the other measurements.

1 cup

1 pint = 2 cups

½ pint = 1 cup

Now Tim can measure the water in the orange bottle with a tool.

Which tool should he pick?

The one cup tool might be too small. He picks the one that measures up to four cups.

He had 2½ cups (0.6 liter) of water in his sport bottle.

Tim's sister didn't go on the walk because she has a sore throat. Mom needs to give her a spoonful of medicine.

Will any spoon do?

No. The wrong amount of medicine could be harmful. The directions say 1 teaspoon (5 milliliters). Mom measures. A teaspoon is not even as much as one swallow.

15

The next day, Tim's sister is feeling better. She and Tim can paint. Tim wants to use orange, but he has none. Mom says to mix red and yellow in equal parts.

Tim mixes ½ cup (118 mL) each of red and yellow paint. Now he's got 1 cup (237 mL) of orange!

Now Tim knows how to measure. He can measure the milk for hot chocolate. He needs 6 fluid ounces (177 mL) of milk.

Tim uses the ounces marks to measure.

18

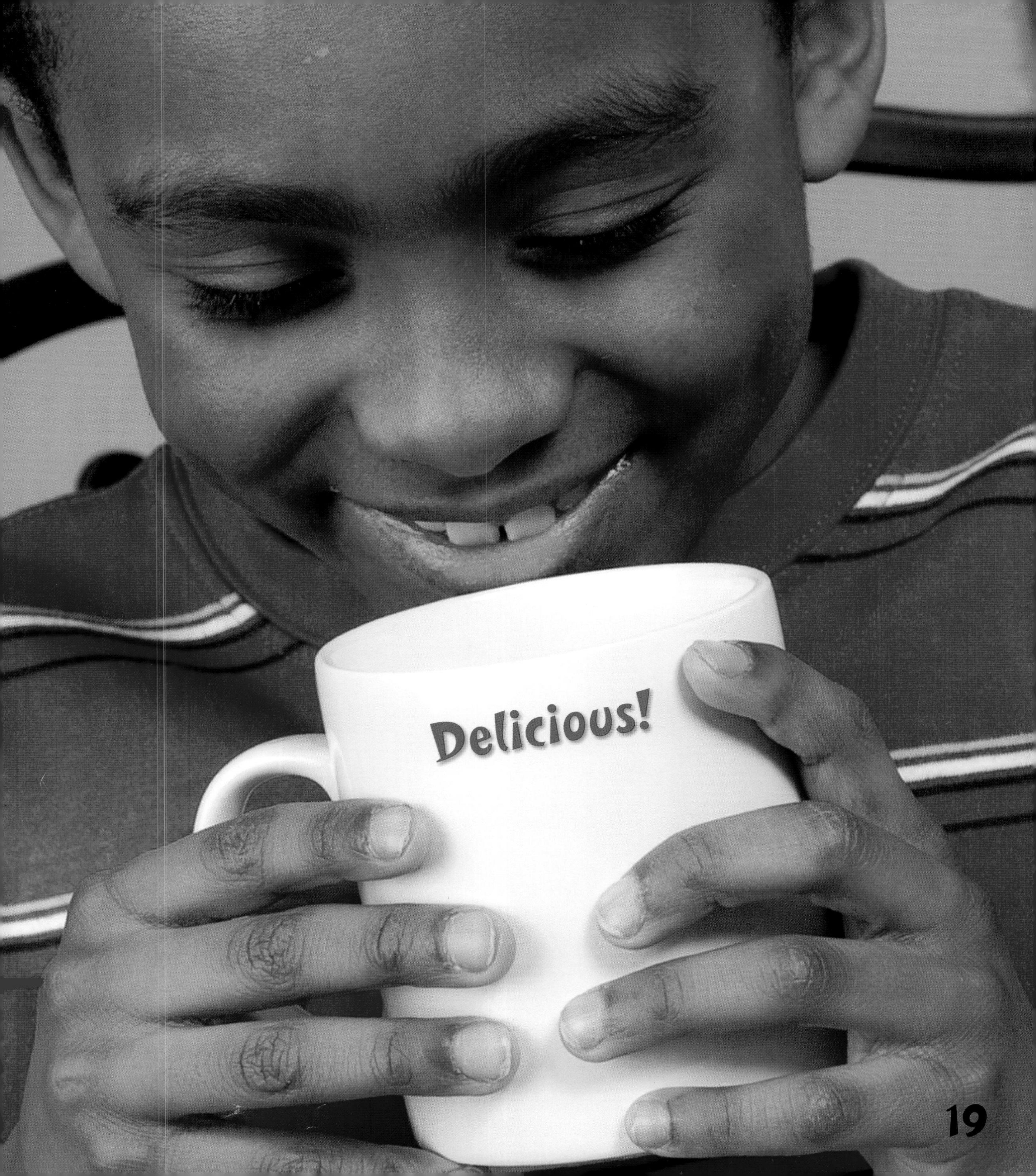

Delicious!

In the morning, Mom asks Tim to make juice.

The directions say to use 2 quarts (1.9 liters) of water. Tim fills the pitcher to the 2-quart line on the side.

A quick stir,
and he's done!

2 quarts

1 quart

Now it's chore time. The fish tank needs more water. How much?

one gallon

half-gallon

22

Tim starts by filling up a 1-gallon (3.8-L) container of water. Then he sees how much of 1 gallon fits in the tank.

It took ½ gallon (1.9 L) of water!

Tim's trying to save water. Does a shower or a bath use more water? Tim plugged the drain when he took his shower. He scooped the water into 5-gallon (19-L) pails.

Tim scooped out 3 pails. That's 15 gallons (57 L).

24

His sister used 20 gallons (76 L) for her bath.

The shower used less water.

With the right tools, you can measure all kinds of liquids.

Buddy got a new dog dish.

Who gets more water now?

Fun Facts about Liquid

• The world's largest fish tank is at the Georgia Aquarium in Atlanta. It holds 6.3 million gallons (23.8 million L) of water. Two whale sharks and many other fish swim in it.

• The average dairy cow produces 7 gallons (26 L) of milk a day.

• To help make all that milk, cows drink up to 50 gallons (189 L) of water each day.

• The United States uses about 380 million gallons (1.4 billion L) of gas each day.

• People use about 2 gallons (7.6 L) of water per minute during a shower.

• Kids take in about 2 quarts (1.9 L) of fluid a day, from both food and drinks. Most people get enough fluid from eating food, drinking with meals, and just drinking when they are thirsty.

• The world's largest swimming pool is in Chile. It contains 66 million gallons (250 million L) of water and covers 20 acres (8 hectares).

Glossary

container—an object that holds something; a measuring cup is a container

cup—a unit of measure equal to 8 fluid ounces; a cup can also mean a small container for holding liquids

fluid ounce—a unit of measure for liquids that is equal to 2 tablespoons or $\frac{1}{16}$ pint

gallon—a unit of measure for liquids that is equal to 4 quarts

level—flat and even

liquid—a wet substance that can be poured

measure—to find out the size of something

metric system—a system of measurement based on counting by 10s; milliliters and liters are basic units of measuring liquid in the metric system

pint—a unit of measure equal to a half quart or 16 fluid ounces

quart—a unit of measure equal to 32 fluid ounces or 2 pints

tablespoon—a unit of measure equal to 3 teaspoons or 0.5 fluid ounce

teaspoon—a unit of measure equal to $\frac{1}{3}$ tablespoon

Read More

Boothroyd Jennifer. *What Is a Liquid?* First Step Nonfiction. Minneapolis: Lerner Publications Co., 2007.

Doudna, Kelly. *Let's Be Kids and Measure Liquids.* Science Made Simple. Edina, Minn.: Abdo Pub. Co., 2007.

Karapetkova, Holly. *Teaspoons, Tablespoons, and Cups.* Measuring. Vero Beach, Fla.: Rourke Publishing, 2010.

Internet Sites

FactHound offers a safe, fun way to find Internet sites related to this book. All of the sites on FactHound have been researched by our staff.

Here's all you do:

Visit *www.facthound.com*

Type in this code: 9781429644570

Index

A+ Books are published by Capstone Press,
151 Good Counsel Drive, P.O. Box 669, Mankato, Minnesota 56002.
www.capstonepub.com

Books published by Capstone Press are manufactured with
paper containing at least 10 percent post-consumer waste.

Library of Congress Cataloging-in-Publication Data
Adamson, Thomas K., 1970–
  How do you measure liquids? / by Thomas K. and Heather
Adamson.
    p. cm. — (A+ books. Measure it!)
  Summary: "Simple text and color photographs describe the
units and tools used to measure liquids"—Provided by publisher.
  Includes bibliographical references and index.
  ISBN 978-1-4296-4457-0 (library binding)
  ISBN 978-1-4296-6331-1 (paperback)
  1. Liquids—Juvenile literature. 2. Volume (Cubic content)—
Juvenile literature. 3. Units of measurement—Juvenile literature.
I. Adamson, Heather, 1974– II. Title. III. Series.
  QC104.A33 2011
  530.8'1—dc22   2010002812

Credits
Gillia Olson, editor; Juliette Peters, designer; Sarah Schuette,
    photo studio specialist; Marcy Morin, studio scheduler;
    Laura Manthe, production specialist

Photo Credits
All photos by Capstone Studio: Karon Dubke, except:
Shutterstock: dcwcreations, 28 (bottom left), hardtmuth, 29 (top
left), toroto reaction, 28 (top right)

Note to Parents, Teachers, and Librarians
The Measure It! series uses color photographs and a nonfiction
format to introduce readers to measuring concepts. *How Do
You Measure Liquids?* is designed to be read aloud to a
pre-reader, or to be read independently by an early reader.
Images and narrative promote mathematical thinking by
showing that objects and time have measurable properties, that
comparisons such as longer or shorter can be made between
multiple objects and time-spans, and that there are standard
and non-standard units for measuring. The book encourages
further learning by including the following sections: Fun Facts,
Glossary, Read More, Internet Sites, and Index. Early readers
may need assistance using these features.